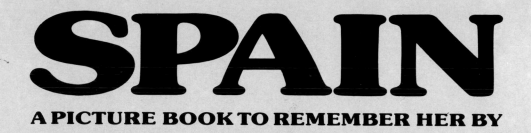

SPAIN

A PICTURE BOOK TO REMEMBER HER BY

Designed by
DAVID GIBBON

Produced by
TED SMART

CRESCENT

INTRODUCTION

Occupying most of the Iberian Peninsula from the Pyrenees to the Strait of Gibraltar, Spain is a country with a rich history, remarkable scenery and a rapidly changing way of life.

Spain's history has been a diverse one. It was inhabited in Pre-Roman days by the Iberians, Celts and Celtiberians and parts of it were colonized by the Phoenicians, Greeks and Carthaginians. The country came under Roman control in 200 B.C. but with the eventual decay of the Roman Empire there followed the deterioration of Spain and the subsequent invasion by the Moors from North-West Africa. The years that followed were turbulent ones, with constant wars between the Moors and Christians, until 1492, when the unification of Spain was accomplished by Ferdinand of Aragon and Isabella of Castile. Under these monarchs – and Charles I and Philip II – Spain became the greatest power in Europe and the ruler of a world-wide empire. The discoveries made by Christopher Columbus, an Italian by birth, were followed by the conquest of most of Central and South America, where today Spanish is the official language of all these countries except Brazil.

However, after the defeat of her Armada by the British in 1558, Spain's power once more began to decline. Wars continued, culminating in the terrible Civil War which began in 1936. Its ending, three years later, saw the start of nearly forty years of rule by General Franco. Since his death Spain has been undergoing an enormous change. The first free parliamentary elections for forty-one years have taken place and it is now a king – Juan Carlos I – who is working towards a new democracy.

History has divided Spain into several regions, Castilian is the official language but Catalan, Euskara and Gallego are also spoken. Each of the regions contains a wide variety of scenery. Surrounding the capital, Madrid, in the centre of the country, is the great Meseta, the arid tableland crossed by wild mountain ranges that prevent the rain from the Atlantic reaching the area. Madrid itself suffered greatly in the Civil War but it has been rebuilt and is now a fine, cosmopolitan city. The famous museum known as the Prado is only one of many in the city, which is also the home of the Escorial, a gloomy building built by Philip II as a palace, monastery and mausoleum combined. Near Madrid lies Toledo with its wealth of Moorish remains, where for centuries the finest sword blades have been forged and where the distinctive gold inlay work introduced by the Moors is still practised.

South east of the Meseta are the fertile fruit-growing regions of Valencia and Murcia. Here, too, is the Costa Blanca, just one of the stretches of coast favoured by European holiday-makers. Only twenty years ago resorts such as Benidorm were sleepy little fishing villages but they have now been transformed into vast holiday complexes of hotels, apartments, discotheques and cafés.

Farther south is Andalusia, the Spain of bullfights, flamenco, guitars and castanets. The sophisticated Costa del Sol, centred around Marbella, with its surfeit of sun, golf and yachts contrasts strongly with inland Andalusia, where whitewashed houses nestle against hillsides, vineyards grow grapes for sherry and fighting bulls are raised in green meadows. Some of the finest bullfights are to be seen in the magnificent cities of Seville and Granada. Spaniards look for artistry as well as bravery in a spectacle that was originally an equestrian tournament in which only noblemen took part. It is still considered the national sport although football is now rapidly gaining in popularity.

Perhaps the most impressive of all Spanish buildings is the Alhambra, a Moorish fortress in Granada, famous for its delicate traceries of filigree stonework. Close by are the beautiful gardens of Generalife, and a gypsy quarter that is a feast of dancing and singing. Rising 12,000 feet above the city is the snow-capped Sierra Nevada, a favourite skiing centre, yet only a short distance from the Mediterranean.

To the west of Granada is Seville, where Sir Francis Drake reputedly 'singed the beard' of the King of Spain. Renowned for its Holy Week procession and its many splendid buildings, Seville also gives its name to the bitter orange which is so essential to the making of marmalade.

Jerez, another Andalusian city, is the heart of the small area where sherry, one of the world's great wines, is produced. Throughout Jerez there are numerous bodegas, the cellars where the grape juice is kept in oak casks to ferment.

From north of Valencia to the French border lies the region of Catalonia. Its capital, Barcelona, is an important industrial city and port, and it boasts one of the oldest shipyards in Europe, the Atarazana, now a naval museum. On a hilltop above Barcelona is the Pueblo Espagnol, a stucco village of facsimiles of the most typical examples of architecture from all over Spain. Down in the city is the Ramblas, where flower and pet markets are held. The scent of roses and carnations perfumes the air and exotic birds sing from their ornate cages, all under a canopy of plane trees. Pablo Picasso spent his youth in Barcelona and there is a fascinating museum, filled with his drawings and paintings, that is a great attraction.

Near Barcelona is the Costa Brava, a part of the coast that has been specifically designed to attract the many thousands of French, British and German tourists who visit it every year. One of the main industries in this area used to be cork processing, and although the cork trees are still to be seen, the factories are either empty, or have been replaced by hotels.

The lesser-known seaside resorts are to be found in the north of Spain, in the Basque Provinces. Here, fine sand beaches are washed by Atlantic rollers and cooled by sea breezes. San Sebastian, reminiscent of Nice or Cannes, is situated here and it was the favourite resort of past kings of Spain.

Inland and into Navarre and Aragon is to be seen the influence of the Pyrenees. The scenery is rugged, with gorges, waterfalls and high, snow-covered peaks surrounding remote mountain villages connected only by winding roads, with knife-edged drops of up to 2,000 feet. This area, in addition to those already mentioned, offers all the ingredients necessary to attract the millions of people who visit Spain every year. Tourism continues to be one of the most important industries and it has been directly responsible for raising the living standards of a truly beautiful country.

The golden glow of sunset *left* shimmers
softly over the Salida de Sol.

Barcelona, the capital of Catalonia, is
an important commercial city, but the
pervading atmosphere is essentially
that of a seaport.

The famous Ramblas, hub of the city,
are constantly alive and full of colour as
this street-market scene *left*, shows.

Calvo Sotelo Plaza *top right* is
renowned for its shops, bars and
restaurants, whilst close by is the wide
tree-lined Paseo de Gracia, *bottom
right.*

A Moorish influence is reflected in the
museum in Guell Park *above,* designed
by the famous architect Antonio Gaudi
y Cornet.

The mountain of Montjuich is seen
centre right with the city shelving
gracefully into the distance and on one
of its slopes stand the Stadium and
Greek Theatre, side by side.
A magnificent panorama of the city
overleaf.

The pillars and spires of Barcelona's
Gothic Cathedral are seen to perfection
when floodlit against a midnight sky
left.

The richly ornate structure of Gaudi's
Cathedral of the Sacred Family *above*,
mercifully escaped destruction during
the Civil War.

Fountains are a special feature of the
city and are particularly splendid at
Montjuich *top right* and outside the
National Palace *below right*.

The flamboyant structure of the San
Pablo Hospital *centre right* lies on the
Avenida Padre Claret.

Beautiful Barcelona, essentially a port,
is seen *overleaf*.

9

Sitges *above and near right* is an old
established seaside resort in Catalonia
province. The town itself has almost an
air of Victoriana about it, with its many
fascinating buildings, whilst safe
bathing from its marvellous beach is
particularly pleasant for holiday
makers.

Tarragona on the Costa Dorada is one of
the most interesting towns in Spain, -
having once been the centre of Roman
power under the name of Tarraco. In
the Plaza del Pallol can be seen the
remains of the Roman forum *above right*
and *below right* are the old Roman
fortifications with their rusting cannon.

14

Lloret de Mar *above and below left* and
Estartit *centre right* are just two of the
many popular holiday resorts on the
Costa Brava. Transformed from sleepy
fishing villages, they now throng with
visitors who fill the prolific hotels,
restaurants and discotheques.

At Palamos *above* the fresh farm
produce awaits the discerning shopper.

Blanes, whose beautiful botanical
gardens can be seen *above right,* is
situated at what is officially the end of
the Costa Brava.

Gerona *below right* is one of the
loveliest cities in Europe with tiered
houses rising above the river Oñar. Its
remarkable Cathedral is three times the
width of Westminster Abbey yet
possesses only one nave.

The whitewashed houses of Palafrugell,
nestling on a sandy beach *overleaf,*
provide an attractive background for
the blue/green Mediterranean waters
lapping the shore.

Dividing France and Spain are the Pyrenean Mountains with their often remote and picturesque villages nestling on the mountainside. Panticosa *above left* with verdant pastures and misty background; Pancorbo *near left* with its desolate mountains and *above right* Lérida, are typical examples.

On the north coast the pretty resort of Elanchove *far left* is contrasted sharply with the industrial city of Bilbao *above*.

19

Segovia, one of Spain's beautiful museum towns, is situated on a hill and the graceful Gothic Alcazar standing in a sea of gold *above,* is sited at the western end.

The magnificent 16th century cathedral *righ and overleaf,* in florid Gothic style dominates the town's centre, whilst the Roman aqueduct *above right* is a well preserved part of Segovia's rich heritage.

Lying in a lush green setting, Salamanca *left* is situated on the right bank of the Rio Tormes.

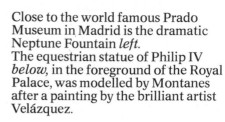

Close to the world famous Prado Museum in Madrid is the dramatic Neptune Fountain *left*.

The equestrian statue of Philip IV *below*, in the foreground of the Royal Palace, was modelled by Montanes after a painting by the brilliant artist Velázquez.

To the north of the Royal Palace are the enclosed Sabatini Gardens *centre left*, laid out in symmetry and elegance. Puerta de Alcala *left* is a monumental arched gateway built in honour of Charles III in 1778 and following this theme, the Plaza Mayor *right,* with its nine arched gateways leading into the great square, has been the scene of countless bullfights and executions.

One of the finest examples of Neo-Classical architecture is the Royal Palace *overleaf.* With its Italianate exterior and superbly furnished French interior it is considered to be one of the most impressive palaces in Europe.

Madrid became the capital of Spain in 1606, at the decree of King Philip II. Like other large cities it has undergone countless changes, particularly during the last fifteen years.

The lovely monument to Cervantes, creator of Don Quixote, is set in the tranquil Plaza de España *below left*, almost overshadowed by one of the tallest skyscrapers in Madrid, which can also be seen *above left* from the Calle de Alcala.

In this rooftop view overlooking the Plaza de España *right* the city sprawls into the distance, making the Plaza a quiet oasis amidst the bustle of everyday life.

The Apollo Fountain *below* is just one of the many beautiful fountains to be found in Madrid.

Cuenca, chief town of its province in New Castile, is also important agriculturally. Built on a craggy promontory the houses *left* can be seen clinging to the hillside in this fascinating town built on an old Roman site. The "Hanging House" *above* teeters dangerously in this most perilous position.

South of Madrid are many picturesque
towns and villages, typical of which is
the Castilian village of Aura *left*.
The whitewashed houses of Munera
above left are massed together beneath
the ruins of an Arab castle, set like a
crown on the hill's summit. The unusual
windmills of Consuegra *above and
below right* stand like sentinels in the
desolate landscape.

Toledo *overleaf*, the ancient capital of
Castile and for many centuries famous
for its fine steel, is situated on a rugged
bluff, surrounded on three sides by the
River Tagus. The highest part of the city
is dominated by the famous ruins of the
Alcazar, which has been a fort, barracks
and royal palace at various stages in its
history.

Andalusia in southern Spain is the home of flamenco, the wild gypsy dance synonymous with Spain. Seville's world famous fair, lasting three days and nights is a most flamboyant occasion with its beautiful horses and colourful costumes, some examples of which can be seen in the pictures on these pages.

To stand in the fields *overleaf* and gaze on the misty hills, one would surely be "drowsed by the fume of poppies".

37

The magnificent Plaza de España, seen on these two pages, with its semi-circular Nash-like façade, houses the Capitania General and lies to the north-east of Maria Luisa's Park; the lovely gardens which have been variously landscaped since the end of the 19th century.

Seville's skyline *overleaf left* reflects a bewildering variety of architectural styles, whilst the lovely Moorish inspired Mudejar Pavilion, in the Plaza America, can be seen *above right*. *Below* is the busy Port of San Telmo with the city laid out neatly beneath a cloudless blue sky.

Cadiz *right,* one of the most ancient towns in the world and fabled to have been founded by Hercules, contains a mixture of modern industrial buildings and old romantic ones. An important port of call on the transatlantic shipping route it is the capital of the province which is the foremost sherry producing area of Spain. Jerez, which gives its name to the most famous of all sherries is a city of old palaces whose bright streets are lined with fragrant orange trees. The picturesque thatched cottages of the district can be seen *left* and *below,* the aromatic vineyards tended lovingly by the careful vine-dresser.

The Costa del Sol ranges the full length of the Mediterranean shoreline of Andalusia and is so called because the sun rarely leaves this paradise which has one of the mildest climates of the region. Marbella *above* and Torremolinos *right*, with their fine sandy beaches and numerous hotels and villas, attract thousands of sun-worshippers each year. Fuengirola, whose beautiful azure harbour can be seen *left* has four miles of beaches to attract visitors, as well as fine sports facilities and a popular yacht club.

The magnificent aerial view of Malaga *overleaf* is dominated by the circular bull-ring and in the background, blue on blue, merge sea and sky.

47

Alhambra *right and below right* is a
city of palaces, whilst the Alhambra
itself, of unique design, is universally
recognised as one of the Wonders of
World.
Influenced greatly by Arabic culture
awe-inspiring Courtyard of Lions *left*
was the last addition of Mohammed V
whose father, Yusuf I, was responsible
for many magnificent reforms and
decorations to this outstanding
monument.

The tranquil Generalife *overleaf* was
once the retreat of the Nazarite Kings;
understandably so, with its beautiful
cypresses and secluded patios. It also
contains an open air theatre which is
used for the International Festival of
Music and Drama.

Poised on a steep grassy hill is the little white town of Vejer de la Frontera *right* whose peaceful square *below* contains a beautiful Moorish inspired fountain. Not far from Vejer, in the vicinity of Casa Viejas can be found some exciting prehistoric caves with murals depicting hunting scenes.

In the region of Alcaudette the green olive groves *left* are as in a chequer-board on the undulating slopes which finally fade into the misty mountains. Also in this rich Andalusian valley, with its vineyards and citrus groves, can be seen the wheat fields *right,* laid out with careful symmetry.

Benidorm on the Costa Blanca is one of the chief centres of international tourism. This modern town *above left*, with its many hotels and apartment blocks lining the blue coastline, is built on the hill of Cnfali. Its growth has been phenomenal, both as a summer and winter resort and its lively night life matches the lights of its skyscrapers seen *below right*.

Calpe *above* lies at the foot of the barren Peñón de Ifach, whose summit can be reached through a tunnel in the rock. This important fishing port has ruins dating back to the time of the Phoenicians and is one of the most popular resorts on the Costa Blanca.

The picturesque resort of Jávea, with its marina, can be seen *left*. It lies at the mouth of the Morach River. The area is renowned for its many caves, some of which can only be reached by sea.

Mallorca (or Majorca) is the largest of the Balearic Islands and its capital, Palma, lying in a magnificent wide bay, holds a wealth of historic interest. Its majestic Gothic cathedral is seen *near left* as dawn rises over the bay. Lovely Illetas *above right* with its fine sandy beaches has pine trees reaching down to the shoreline, whilst Portals Nous *right* is a quiet haven for visitors. *Above left* the sleepy town of Valldemosa nestles in the rugged landscape and *below* in this island of contrasts a farmhand sets about his daily task.

Ibiza is the third largest island in the Balearics, with a rugged coastline jutting into the blue sea *left*. Its splendid pine forests are of particular note and indeed the Greeks once called the island Pitiusa, meaning pine-land. Almond groves, fig trees and palms all combine to scent the air in this blissful island.

Ibiza, the capital of the island, is a pretty seafaring city with steep cobbled streets *above*, lined with elegant white houses. The tranquil scene *below right* with its berthed boats and yachts is a typical one in this lovely island.

Port de Torrent *above right* has white sandy beaches and a sheltered blue bay, making it an obvious favourite with many tourists.

The tiny island of Minorca with its 120 miles of shoreline, has an engaging simplicity which delights all visitors to its shores.

The typical Minorcan farm *centre far right* is set amidst the gently undulating countryside.

The clear air and azure skies of Binibeca *left and top right* with its lovely white-washed houses has a truly universal appeal.

Ciudadela, whose cathedral and harbour can be seen *above,* is a picturesque town lying in a sheltered bay. On the outskirts of the town can be seen the Naveta dels Tudons, the most important of the megalithic structures which are to be found in the area.

Mahon *right* is the capital of the island and has been greatly influenced by English design, particularly noticeable along the waterfront. On the north side of the harbour is the "Golden Farm" where Lady Hamilton and Lord Nelson resided whilst visiting the island.

63

First published in Great Britain 1978 by Colour Library International Ltd.
© Illustrations: Colour Library International Ltd. Colour separations by La Cromolito, Milan, Italy.
Display and text filmsetting by Focus Photoset, London, England.
Printed and bound by L.E.G.O. Vicenza, Italy.
Published by Crescent Books, a division of Crown Publishers Inc.
Library of Congress Catalogue Card No. 77-18465
CRESCENT 1978